Speed Reading

The Definitive Manual For Acquiring Proficiency In Speed Reading And Enhancing Cognitive Recall

(An Instruction Manual For Novices On Enhancing Reading Speed And Comprehension)

Leonid Vinogradov

TABLE OF CONTENT

Speed Reading Defined 1
The Advantages Of Speed Reading 13
Foundational Concepts For Enhanced Cognitive Assimilation 20
How To Determine An Individual's Personality Profile 31
The Importance Of Speed Reading 43
Tools And Techniques 57
Getting Organized 79
The Concept Of Achieving A 300% Increase In Reading Speed Within A Span Of Merely Six Hours 103
Barriers To Speed Reading 126
Comparing Speed Reading And Active Reading 131

Speed Reading Defined

An image conveys a multitude of meanings through visual representation. A single image is worth a thousand words. Nevertheless, when contemplating an image, it is unnecessary to meticulously examine each individual feature such as the eye, the nose, the ears, the long brown hair, and so forth, in order to discern that it represents a face. Similarly, when we engage in reading, it is not imperative for us to individually scrutinize each word and vocalize it in order to comprehend the underlying message conveyed by the collective content. In a manner akin to perceiving an image and rapidly discerning its content, our eyes and cognitive faculties possess the capacity to scan the written words on a single page within a brief span of 5 to 10 seconds, comprehending with full clarity the concept that the words have vividly depicted.

Envision the ability to glance at a single page and comprehend its content within a mere span of 10 seconds. The corollary here suggests that one is capable of comprehensively digesting and analyzing a 350-page literary work within a span of an hour, effectively grasping the content and subsequently expounding upon the concepts or personal reflections with intellectual acuity, thereby demonstrating a comprehensive assimilation of the material and preservation of pertinent information. This encapsulates the fundamental principles of rapid reading.

No singular individual or collective entity possesses exclusive control over the techniques, concepts, and execution of speed reading. The majority of the concepts remain identical, with the divergence lying in the manner in which they are imparted, ultimately determining the outcome of either failure or success. Furthermore, speed reading does not depend on one's intelligence or level of education. However, I am confident that by utilizing this guide, you will greatly enhance your learning ability and expand your knowledge exponentially. However, the ability to read quickly is contingent upon the cessation of ineffective practices, the presence of unwavering commitment, and, naturally, consistent honing of skills through repetitive action. In order to enhance your speed, the essential requirements encompass a reliable set of visual senses (such as a commendable pair of contact lenses or eyeglasses), a suitable timer, the cognitive ability to adhere to instructions, and possession of this book.

Strategies for attaining optimal reading velocities

The acquisition of proficiency in anything novel hinges solely on the diligent application of practice. Temple Grandin's extraordinary abilities in rapid reading and memory recall are evident, distinguishing her from individuals such as yourself and me, who have not inherently acquired the capacity to read beyond 60 pages per minute. Our initial objective is to effectively eliminate detrimental patterns, inherent in all individuals, through a systematic approach which I will duly impart, followed by diligent exercise.

Psychologists refer to the utilization of a scientifically validated approach to enhance speed reading as the development of motor skills. Motor skills are acquired by effectively coordinating physical activities with a given task. It is acquired as an innate ability through consistent practice and unwavering determination, starting from basic tasks such as an infant's process of mastering arm and leg movements, progressing to skills like walking and operating a vehicle, and eventually culminating in more intricate proficiencies such as musical instrument proficiency or becoming an exceptional athlete endowed with superior speed and jumping ability beyond that of the average person. Undoubtedly, these skills are acquired through rigorous training and consistent practice.

The significance of fine motor skills cannot be overstated when it comes to achieving success in speed reading. This is primarily due to the fact that speed reading comprises exercises that effectively train and refine the eye's ability to swiftly scan and comprehend text at accelerated rates. In contrast to professional athletes and musical prodigies, the skill of speed reading does not necessitate extensive daily practice sessions to enhance reading speeds. Indeed, the provided book offers straightforward exercises that can aid in improving your words per minute within a brief timeframe. To unlock the gate to attaining your utmost capability, it is imperative to engage in daily practice sessions lasting less than half an hour. The objective is to instill these reading habits deeply within your mind so that, akin to the automaticity achieved in activities such as driving, walking, and cycling, they are performed effortlessly.

Do not lose hope if you find yourself incapable of performing the drills on a daily basis. Engage in this activity thrice a week or as per your personal feasibility. By performing these exercises just once, it is guaranteed that you will unconsciously engage in focused practice, leading to an notable enhancement in your speed. Please be reminded that there is no requirement for continued self-instruction pertaining to driving, walking, or riding a bicycle. The exercises are of such elementary nature that once grasp, there is no necessity to repetitively revisit them. One must, in a manner reminiscent of Nike's tagline, confidently take action.

The Advantages of Speed Reading" or "The Beneficial Aspects of Speed Reading

Thus far, the analysis has centered on the process of reading, including the techniques necessary for effective Speed Reading. This chapter will elucidate the advantages individuals stand to gain from the practice of Speed Reading. Speed Reading is not merely a practice focused on reading at a rapid pace, but rather a proficiency that enhances the reader's capacity for comprehension. It is intricately linked to the fundamental comprehension of the concepts elucidated within the text. The primary benefit of speed reading lies in its ability to allow the reader to acquire a significantly greater amount of information within a designated timeframe, in contrast with an individual who reads at an average pace.

Swift Understanding

In order for the brain to achieve optimum performance, it is imperative to consistently engage in training. Consider a video game that encompasses various levels. The human brain requires a period of adjustment to acclimate to the given circumstances. The speed reading skill follows a similar pattern where enhancement is achieved through a variety of exercises, leading to an elevated level of comprehension resulting from consistent practice and rigorous engagement. When chosen with careful consideration, speed reading exercises facilitate enhanced comprehension of the text whilst maintaining the pace.

Confidence

It is customary for individuals to form judgments when an individual begins to express themselves orally. Speed reading provides the reader with numerous advantages in a minimal amount of time. It is advantageous for individuals with greater reading speed to extensively peruse written material in order to enhance their preparedness for a meeting, discussion, or presentation when compared to individuals with more typical reading speeds. By adopting this approach, the speed reader ensures that they remain within their comfort zone while disseminating novel ideas, facts, and information pertaining to any given subject. It exerts a favorable influence on one's character and concurrently enhances one's self-assurance. Certainly, after extensively studying a particular subject, an individual will possess a substantial amount of knowledge and logical reasoning to effectively communicate when speaking to a group.

Sharp Memory

Engaging in the practice of speed reading enhances cognitive functions such as memory and the capacity to absorb and retain substantial amounts of factual knowledge. Memory is directly connected to the capacity for comprehension and an enhanced aptitude for understanding. The brain functions optimally in preserving information within its memory stores. Additionally, memory plays a pivotal role among the various factors influencing creativity, as it is a heightened memory capacity that fosters innovative thinking.

Neuroplasticity

Neuroplasticity pertains to the brain's capacity to establish connections between disparate concepts. It enables individuals to synergistically incorporate diverse concepts, thereby facilitating the formulation of logical conclusions. Engaging in accelerated reading techniques enhances the neuroplasticity of the human brain. It facilitates enhanced cognitive processing, expedites effective decision-making, facilitates logical deductions, fosters concept integration, and promotes ingenious thinking. This attribute allows the adept speed reader to distinguish themselves in their professional endeavors.

Improved Focus

The skill of rapid reading allows the reader to sustain their concentration on the written material. Over time, through the application of diligent practice and unwavering consistency, the human mind becomes acclimated to directing its attention towards the crucial objective in question, thereby forsaking any propensity towards diverting distractions. Concentration is regarded as a hallmark of excellence among office professionals. The absence of focus invariably results in errors and has a detrimental effect on an individual's character.

The Advantages Of Speed Reading

After acquiring the skill of speed-reading, one will come to recognize the considerable advantages it offers, leading to an enhanced sense of intellect and discernment. When one effectively optimizes the acquisition of knowledge within a minimal temporal framework, it engenders a heightened inclination to pursue further reading and intellectual enrichment. Furthermore, your aptitude for comprehension will be honed.

Speed reading encompasses more than simply reading faster. It concerns enhancing one's comprehension and ability to retain information over an extended period of time. Proficiently practicing the art of rapid reading lends itself as an exceptional technique to enhance the cognitive aptitude, thereby providing opportunities to explore uncharted potentials through the utilization of accelerated neural activity and increased temporal resources.

It will provide you with the opportunity to remain abreast and well-informed in this fiercely competitive realm, thereby expanding your scope of understanding. By engaging in speed reading, one can indeed enhance their cognitive processing capabilities and capacity for effective retention of information. One has the potential to attain significant popularity in any given setting, akin to the character of Bradley Cooper in the film Limitless.

Benefits

"There are numerous additional advantages, which include:

You Improve Your Memory

The brain can be likened to a muscle, as it exhibits improved performance through training, much like other muscles within the human body. It will experience enhanced growth and demonstrate superior performance. Speed reading is a methodology that enhances cognitive development and elevates cognitive performance. By enhancing the capacity of your brain to process information at an accelerated rate, various cognitive aspects, such as memory function, become enhanced. The memory operates akin to a stabilizing muscle that is engaged during the process of rapid reading.

You attain an enhanced level of concentration.

While the majority of individuals possess a reading speed of approximately 200 words per minute, there exists a subset of individuals who have the ability to read upwards of 300 words per minute. The initial factor is their disassociation from the traditional approach to reading, imparted to us all, as it is substantiated that it is arguably the most ineffectual method to comprehend and acquire knowledge. Furthermore, it is often the case that the typical individual exhibits a lack of attentiveness.

During the act of reading, it is common for our minds to stray and engage in introspection. Thus, it may appear as though you are engaged in the act of reading, but in actuality, you are not. Speed reading addresses this issue and enhances your capacity for concentration and attention.

Increases Your Self-Confidence

It is often the case that you possess the highest level of intelligence and extensive knowledge amongst the individuals present in the room. This is usually the result of being able to learn anything from any walk of life faster once you can read and comprehend at super-human speeds. Enhancing your aptitude to comprehend and assimilate information expeditiously broadens your horizons and engenders a multitude of possibilities for personal advancement.

One gains a comprehensive understanding, enabling the interpretation and analysis of matters at a more profound level of consciousness. Irrespective of whether you engage in reading works of fiction or non-fiction, the act of speed-reading will undeniably contribute to your personal growth and aptitude enhancement. Through the acquisition of a higher level of understanding and perceptiveness, one can experience a substantial enhancement in self-assurance.

You Acquire Better Logical Skills

Engaging in reading is highly beneficial for enhancing cognitive ability. It cultivates enhanced reading speed and fosters cognitive efficiency in processing and integrating information, thereby facilitating the identification of correlations between stored knowledge and incoming information. This facilitates the process of drawing analogies and deciphering events that exhibit resemblance, thereby enhancing your aptitude for problem-solving.

As one engages in dedicated practice to enhance reading speed, the progression of this process accelerates, leading to an automatic improvement in logical thinking. Gradually, individuals become accustomed to swiftly responding to tasks that previously consumed significant time and effort.

You Grow Emotionally

Engaging in the act of reading has the potential to stimulate the release of endorphins, which are neurotransmitters associated with feelings of joy and euphoria, resulting in an enhanced state of happiness and cognitive brightness. Engaging in activities that divert your attention from concerns and daily pressures, including those thoughts that are detrimental to your well-being, serves to alleviate stress. When engaging in the practice of rapid reading, it becomes evident that an individual's level of absorption in the material significantly intensifies, fostering a heightened sense of connection with the content at hand.

This naturally enhances your level of concentration on the material you peruse. This phenomenon can alternatively be referred to as 'active-meditation', denoting a reflective state that can be attained through engaging in an activity, specifically, speed-reading. This facilitates the alleviation of tension and enhances your emotional well-being.

Foundational Concepts For Enhanced Cognitive Assimilation

There exist fundamental principles of speed reading that serve as guiding factors in the reading process, and it is imperative to ascertain one's purpose prior to commencing the exercise. In order to adequately ready oneself for the act of reading, it is imperative to possess a thorough comprehension of the intended objective behind the reading process, while concurrently fostering a desirable mental disposition. If your intention in reading is to meet an assignment's requirements, it is improbable that you will retain a significant amount of the information as you are more prone to merely skim through the book in search of answers to the given questions.

Enhanced reading comprehension can be achieved when one's reading objectives are well-defined, and the subsequent elucidation presents a range of key motivations behind individuals' engagement in reading activities.

To possess a thorough understanding of a specific piece of information.

Conducting an investigation to acquire crucial information

To answer specific questions

To assess the contents of the material being perused. To analyze the information being consumed. To appraise the substance of the text being examined.

Engaging in literary pursuits for recreational purposes Indulging in the act of reading for personal enjoyment or amusement Pursuing the pleasurable activity of reading for leisure or entertainment

Engaging in the application of the concepts gained during the learning process.

Developing a clear objective for one's reading is a fundamental prerequisite for achieving full understanding of the text. While engaging in the act of reading, it is imperative to contemplate the content being read with regards to the desired objective one intends to achieve. The results can be classified into the following categories:

Engaging in an in-depth reading process with the explicit goal of assimilating the material into one's memory.

Reading with the purpose of gaining a comprehensive understanding of the topic.

Engaging in literature analysis with the purpose of bolstering an argument or gathering substantiating evidence.

Engaging in focused reading for the purpose of providing answers on a specific subject

Engaging in deliberate reading with the objective of obtaining a diverse array of viewpoints pertaining to a particular topic.

Engaging in literature with the primary objective of obtaining precise data and factual information.

The intended objective of reading or the anticipated result thus determines the approach to be employed for reading, leading to the attainment of optimal comprehension levels. As previously indicated, the primary objective of this book is not solely to enhance the velocity at which you read, but also to elevate your capacity for comprehension and retention of the material being read. In order to bring about the actualization of this objective, it is imperative to engage in active reading, which entails demonstrating awareness of the intended purpose of reading as well as mentally and emotionally engaging with the content being communicated.

Adopting a focused mindset while reading additionally aids in mitigating distractions that frequently result in reduced reading velocity. When one's envisioned objective becomes evident, it facilitates greater precision and engenders a heightened capacity for undivided concentration. The establishment of a clear objective in one's reading fosters a conducive cognitive state, facilitating the comprehension and recall of the information being read.

Comprehension versus Retention

A thorough understanding and effective retention are critical components needed to achieve the desired outcome associated with comprehending a particular subject matter. Comprehension may be delineated as the degree to which one grasps and assimilates a subject matter upon initial reading, whereas retention pertains to the faculty of recollecting and retaining knowledge acquired from prior reading. Suppose, for instance, that you are engaged in reading a book and are able to articulate your understanding of the passage you have perused—an act commonly referred to as comprehension. Retention refers to the ability to recall information when queried about your reading at a later point in time. The information that is at your disposal is what you have successfully preserved.

An additional illustration of retention can be demonstrated by considering a scenario wherein one is faced with an examination on a subject previously studied. In this case, an individual may recognize familiarity with the topic and recall having studied it before, yet unfortunately find themselves unable to recall the specific answer. This occurrence signifies a suboptimal level of retention regarding the material that was read. While you demonstrated understanding while perusing the subject matter, you were unable to effectively retain the acquired information. An individual may possess a notable level of understanding, yet exhibit shortcomings in the aspect of memory retention. It is imperative to address this particular area in order to achieve overall success in the pursuit of speed reading.

When engaged in the discipline of speed reading, numerous individuals experience apprehension regarding the potential oversight of certain words, as they harbor the concern that incomplete recognition of letters may impede their comprehension of the text. The utmost significance lies in the capacity to comprehend written content, a feat attainable through a comprehensive grasp of the workings of the human brain.

In order to enhance both comprehension and retention, the subsequent exercise can be highly beneficial.

"The exercise of reading and remembering:

This activity entails the perusal of a paragraph followed by the act of making concise records, which is to be continued consistently throughout the entirety of the reading material. The annotations you make on the paragraph should be concise and avoid providing an extensive summary of the content. The appropriate term should merely encapsulate the content that has been read within the paragraph. It is also imperative that you consistently inquire within yourself about the content you have recently perused.

By making careful annotations of the main ideas presented in the paragraph and consistently engaging in self-inquiry regarding your understanding of the material, you will enhance both your level of comprehension and capacity for retaining the information. The exercise demonstrates a potential for sustained practice, resulting in enhanced recall capacity. With persistent practice over the course of several weeks, proficiency in this exercise transforms into an ingrained habit. One of the primary causes of poor information retention among readers is their lack of attentiveness to the content they are reading.

The read and recall method of reading is a methodology that allows individuals to enhance their attentiveness and retention while reading, achieved through the practice of taking notes and actively engaging in questioning during the process. One of the most straightforward methods that can be employed to enhance comprehension entails modifying the pace at which one reads. In order to improve understanding, one may opt to decelerate while reading the initial sentence of a paragraph, and subsequently increase the reading pace as progress is made.

In the majority of instances, the initial sentence of a paragraph is indicative of the central theme encompassed by the whole paragraph. By deliberately reading it at a slower pace, one can effectively gain an understanding and comprehension of the subject matter being discussed. Upon perusing the information, you will observe an acceleration in comprehension for certain sentences as your pace of understanding improves for others. This particular methodology of reading facilitates the preservation of comprehension, as it allows for a harmonious balance between the pace of reading and the attainment of the desired level of understanding. It is unfeasible to maintain a consistently high reading speed and yet achieve the intended level of comprehension.

How To Determine An Individual's Personality Profile

Initially, let us examine the insights that can be gleaned from an individual's outward appearance. An initial observation one may make pertains to an individual's level of self-care. If an individual takes proper care of their personal well-being, they will don tidy attire and observe fundamental practices of personal hygiene. To illustrate, it is likely that their hair and teeth will be properly groomed. They shall be attired in presentable, immaculate garments too.

Another observation that can be made regarding an individual's appearance is their level of self-assurance. If individuals exhibit postural inconsistencies such as slouching or avoiding direct eye contact with individuals in their vicinity, it could indicate a potential unease or lack of self-assurance within the specific context they find themselves in. This observation could indicate either a tendency towards introversion or a high degree of sensitivity. One will discern their type based on other traits observed in them.

One may also observe an individual's choice of words as one engages in conversation with them, or even when hearing them speak from a distance. If an individual employs extensive and intricate vocabulary, it is likely indicative of their value for education or an intention to project professionalism in their professional sphere. Their lexicon can additionally aid in classifying them into specific character profiles. If an individual engages in extensive verbal communication and exhibits a propensity for verbosity, it is likely indicative of extroversion, leading to a reasonable assumption of their normal temperament rather than a high sensitivity level. Should they persist in engaging in positive communication with individuals in their vicinity, one could plausibly deduce that they exhibit a stronger propensity to respond favorably to affirmative language and commendations.

Subsequently, it is conceivable that you can acquire further insights into the character traits of individuals whom you are speed reading by considering their vocation. If an individual is engaged in a profession that necessitates addressing sizable gatherings or interacting with clients throughout the day, and they display a genuine affinity for such activities, it is likely indicative of their extroverted nature. If the individual in question is a counselor who deeply values engaging in conversations about clients' emotions and mental well-being, it is reasonable to infer that they exhibit a heightened level of sensitivity or possess a disposition that leans towards feelings as opposed to rational thinking. If they hold a high-level position in a sizable corporation, it is possible to discern their inclination towards dominance when assessing these personality assessments.

An additional factor to consider in an individual is their level of education. Individuals who possess a master's degree and demonstrate a genuine passion for acquiring knowledge may exhibit a predisposition towards cognitive analysis rather than emotional considerations. They may also exhibit a tendency towards conscientiousness, as well as a strong inclination to be mindful of the emotions and perspectives of others.

Identifying the person's areas of interest can assist you in efficiently understanding their mindset and gaining insights into their character. Should they possess an affinity for embracing gestures, they may exhibit a preference for expressing affection through tactile means. If their primary focus is exploring the world alongside their companions, they may find solace in dedicating quality time to this pursuit. Should they display a preference for solitude or engage in solitary pursuits, it is plausible to infer their disposition as either introverted or highly sensitive, contingent upon their other discernible qualities to establish precise categorization.

The vocal intonation of an individual can provide valuable insights into their character and personality. If individuals display signs of mellowness and seclusion, it is likely indicative of their introverted nature, heightened sensitivity, or both. If individuals consistently exhibit a manner of speaking that conveys a perception of emotional distress caused by your words or actions, it is likely indicative of them being highly sensitive individuals. If they communicate with a boisterous, amiable, and effervescent manner, it is likely that they possess extraverted tendencies and display little to no signs of being highly sensitive. If their manner of communication reflects a keen understanding of your innermost emotions, they could be deemed intuitive. If they communicate devoid of any affect and sentiment, it is possible that their level of sensitivity may fall below that of the average individual.

When endeavoring to gain deeper insights into an individual's true character through attentive listening, it is crucial to go beyond the mere verbatim content of their speech. It is crucial to listen to their vocal inflections and observe their nonverbal cues.

As a case in point, during social outings with friends, I frequently engage in an earnest observance of the nonverbal cues exhibited by my companions. Occasionally, the dialogue progresses seamlessly, enabling us to engage in conversation until the early hours. On other occasions, the exchange appears to come to a halt, regardless of the various subjects I attempt to introduce.

Now, I have the option to become displeased by this situation or infer that the other individual is exhibiting aloofness in this context. Alternatively, I could thoroughly examine my acquaintance, as well as my friend, to ascertain if there may be underlying factors contributing to the situation. Is my acquaintance engaging in direct eye contact with me, or are they intentionally evading my presence? Are they smiling or do they seem stressed out? What insights can I gain from observing their posture, tone of voice, and even the orientation of their body?

Frequently, I am able to acquire significant knowledge from observing the nonverbal cues of individuals in my vicinity. On numerous occasions, my friends will experience a sense of relief as they realize that someone has discerned the presence of an issue and is amenable to discussing it.

Let us examine the impact of adopting a studious approach rather than a reactive one. On a particular occasion, I accompanied a gathering of acquaintances and observed a distinct sense of discontent emanating from one individual among us, whom I shall refer to as John. He wore a scowl, his arms tightly wrapped around his body, displaying profound irritation towards his surroundings and the people present.

The remaining individuals within the group began to observe that he was not engaging in conversation and commenced in teasing and investigating him lightly. However, they dismissed it with amusement and did not pursue the matter beyond that. They presumed that he was merely exhibiting a negative disposition and intentionally attempting to further dampen the ambiance.

However, I was aware that there existed an underlying aspect, one that necessitated investigation in order to assist him in breaking free from his inhibitions and genuinely embracing the evening. Therefore, I discreetly spoke with John in a private setting and proceeded to inquire about several matters. Shortly thereafter, John began expressing his discontent towards a colleague who made an attempt to claim credit for his own contributions in the workplace. This single occurrence was nearly sufficient to expose John to potential repercussions in his professional setting. Considering his responsibilities as the provider for his spouse and children, he felt annoyed and lacked the inclination to engage in social activities.

Upon acquiring comprehension of the issue at hand, I gained the ability to wield authority. We departed and embarked on a leisurely stroll, distancing ourselves from the clamor and frivolity that would only exacerbate such a mood. Following a productive conversation, during which we shared a few lighthearted moments to alleviate some of the tension, John was able to return to his family with a profound sense of relief and diminished stress.

In general, it is evident that a multitude of factors contribute to the assessment of an individual's personality. One cannot solely depend on the act of listening to the individual's words. It is imperative to consider their outward presentation, lexical repertoire, professional background, educational attainment, and areas of personal interest. It is imperative to attentively observe both verbal and non-verbal cues such as body language and tone of voice while listening to others, in order to verify the veracity of their statements and determine whether there is any concealed information.

Allow us to engage in an additional activity to reinforce our comprehension of the concepts covered in this chapter. The quiz will be found on the subsequent page. Please respond to the questions in order to ascertain the significance of the traits with respect to the individual's personality. In this context, there exists no definitive correctness or incorrectness, thus, I encourage you to contemplate these ideas and explore their relevance to your own experiences.

Amanda has a strong inclination to arrive at work ahead of schedule and prolong her stay in order to engage in conversations with her colleagues. She articulates her thoughts with a resounding voice and exudes an unwavering aura of assurance, perpetually adorned with a genial countenance in the midst of discourse. What are the personality types possessed by Amanda and what is the rationale behind them?

Richard is a man of integrity. He diligently applies himself, despite harboring aversion towards his occupation. He frequently exhibits episodes of anger during working hours, and upon returning home, he seeks solitude for the duration of the evening. What are Rich's personality types and what is the rationale behind them?

Marshal is the overseer of a labor-intensive establishment. He conducts four daily patrols around the premises to ascertain optimal performance of the manufacturing personnel. He regards himself as being of higher status in comparison to them. What kind of personality attribute does Marshal possess, and what is the reason for this characteristic?

Janna exhibits introverted tendencies. She exhibits contentment and demonstrates exceptional competence in her role; however, she exhibits reticence when it comes to addressing the group in a professional setting. During her designated lunch period, she chooses to dine in solitude as a means of taking a respite from interpersonal engagements. What is the specific personality classification attributed to Janna and what factors contribute to this categorization?

The Importance Of Speed Reading

Speed reading can yield numerous benefits in various aspects. Naturally, my words alone do not suffice as evidence, but extensive research spanning several decades has diligently examined the methods and principles behind effective reading practices. As mentioned earlier, the concept of speed reading entails the ability to accomplish the aforementioned task, thus proving its versatility and practicality in multiple contexts. This chapter elucidates the advantages of speed reading, including ones that could be anticipated as well as those that may be unexpectedly eye-opening.

It facilitates time-saving

I consistently emphasize the notion that contemporary society operates at a rapid pace, for it is imperative to bear this in mind. Moreover, it is essential that we recognize the ramifications of such a fast-paced world. In the midst of our rapidly-evolving and high-pressure society, an imperative to accomplish tasks more expeditiously has emerged, and the imperative to innovate stems from this obligation. Considering that humans possess a natural inclination towards investigating pertinent matters in this present era, it elucidates the likely rationale behind the focus of this research.

Each and every one of us naturally desires the opportunity for an increased allocation of time, harboring the notion that, were the duration of a day to exceed the customary 24 hours, we would undoubtedly accomplish the entirety of our predetermined tasks within that given timeframe.

Regrettably, we are unable to allocate the necessary time, thereby augmenting the value of the time we do have in our lives.

Furthermore, our understanding of reading has evolved in accordance with the nature of our contemporary society. It has become increasingly challenging to allocate time for textual engagement as a casual pursuit – a trend that has resulted in a complete abandonment of reading by individuals. Speed reading eliminates the notion that one lacks the time for reading by effectively demonstrating how one can acquire a greater volume of knowledge within a compressed timeframe. This successfully fulfills a pivotal objective pursued by technological advancements in the realm of human existence. It provides individuals with additional time to allocate according to their own discretion. Indeed, although time machines or portals have not yet been brought into existence by us, it holds true that if we manage to allocate time toward pursuing our desires, the outcome would be just as favorable, would it not?

It enhances the efficiency of your learning journey.

Considering the frequent availability of language in its written form, a vast reservoir of knowledge is made accessible through the written word, which can be accessed by each and every one of us through the act of reading.

Speed reading is, indeed, an advanced form of comprehension, and it is reasonable to assert that this relationship extends to the process of acquiring knowledge. Consequently, speed reading also elevates one's ability to learn. The inherent essence of rapid text comprehension necessitates one's ability to grasp information presented at an accelerated pace, leading to expedited learning within a compressed timeframe.

Moreover, this will enhance your abilities as a learner, as you gradually apprehend the exact components necessary to optimize the efficiency of the learning process. By engaging in speed reading, you will come to comprehend that dedicating extensive hours to reading does not necessarily result in acquiring significantly greater knowledge. There exist expeditious and more effective methods for accomplishing the task. Expertise is contingent upon the depth of knowledge one possesses and the ability to promptly access and apply it. Speed

reading accomplishes that very purpose. Through implementing more effective information management strategies, one can simultaneously enhance their learning and comprehension of the acquired information.
It aids in the efficient execution of multiple tasks simultaneously.
To synthesize the aforementioned claim concisely in a more formal tone: "Undoubtedly, endeavors that effectively economize time yield multifaceted and advantageous outcomes." Speed reading is a task that essentially allows for multitasking capabilities. While it is expected that you abstain from pursuing other tasks while speed reading, it is evident that the advantages extend beyond the act of speed reading itself. While possessing the skill of speed reading is indeed advantageous, the ability to multitask is of paramount importance as it necessitates one's aptitude in managing multiple tasks simultaneously.
This is feasible due to the inherent nature of speed reading, which

necessitates a certain level of multitasking, though it entails more subconscious processes. When engaged in speed reading, one assimilates information, thereby broadening their scope of knowledge, transcending the mere act of sequentially reading words. This transferable skill aids in optimizing the allocation of energy towards other tasks. Furthermore, the practice of speed reading can enhance productivity by efficiently completing reading assignments, resulting in the allocation of surplus time to accomplish other targeted tasks. Considering the efficiency of speed reading, whereby it allows you to accomplish tasks in approximately a quarter of the time taken for conventional reading, you will be left with a surplus of time to dedicate towards other responsibilities.

It aids in enhancing your ability to maintain focus and concentration.

It is imperative for me to emphasize the significance of having a focused attention span. As an illustration, let us consider the following scenario: At present, the only sentence at my disposal is "A dancing penguin was running around in New York." Remarkably, you may notice that your mind readily conjures up this visual representation, even in the absence of any explicit request. This does not inherently indicate any deficiency in your reading abilities. However, the presence of numerous distractions can impede your focus, resulting in decreased efficiency and productivity. This is where the practice of speed reading proves advantageous, as it trains individuals to direct their attention in distinct and beneficial ways.

There are several benefits associated with this. Initially, as your capacity to focus improves, you will acquire the skill to process information with enhanced efficiency and in a condensed timeframe. Consequently, it is imperative that you dedicate a reduced amount of time towards fixating on potential sources of distraction. Furthermore, this capacity to effectively focus your attention in specific manners significantly influences your current interaction and involvement with the surrounding environment. Considering that you are diligently training your mind to enhance your attention span, you will come to acknowledge that directing your focus towards something becomes a less arduous endeavor. This practice not only contributes to significant improvement in reading skills, but also enhances communication abilities in various social contexts, which is an inevitable aspect of human interaction.

It enhances your cognitive abilities.

In order to elucidate the impact of speed reading on cognitive processes, it is imperative to revisit the differentiation initially established between speed reading and fast reading. Considering the distinct objectives of these two skills, it significantly influences how the presented information is cognitively processed. When engaging in the practice of speed reading, it is important to recognize that the objective extends beyond mere reading. It encompasses the aspects of retaining information and being able to recall it as needed.

This is where your knowledge stored in the semantic memory comes into play. Semantic memory pertains to the cognitive storage of factual knowledge, necessitating its enhancement while engaging in accelerated reading techniques. The correlation between rapid reading and comprehension is of utmost importance. The consistent demand for speed reading persists due to its ability to enhance cognitive retention rather than mere short-term assimilation of information.

Moreover, you may observe that speed reading elicits engagement with your memory via multiple channels of input. Indeed, while you engage in the act of comprehension, analysis, and retention of knowledge within your mind, you are simultaneously perceiving words as visual stimuli, thereby facilitating the encoding process through multiple modalities. This, in turn, enhances the ability to retrieve information as needed, as two avenues are now accessible for this cognitive process. Additionally, these sensory associations serve to enhance the associations we possess for specific types of information.

It contributes to the enhancement of cognitive capabilities on a broader scale. Upon considering the cumulative impact of the aforementioned advantages associated with speed reading, one will come to acknowledge that this comprehensive enhancement is hardly a revelation, as it bestows advantages upon various domains of advanced cognitive functions. One manner in which this phenomenon occurs is by means of the neural connections that are established within the brain. It is a fundamental principle in the field of neuroscience that the utilization of a particular neural network leads to the reinforcement of the synaptic connections along that specific pathway. The interactive aspect of speed reading necessitates active involvement with multiple areas of the brain on a frequent basis, leading to an enhancement in overall cognitive capabilities. The inherent familiarity of the neural connections and networks facilitates this process.

Conversely, it exerts an influence on your cognitive functioning by altering your overall psychological well-being. An extensive body of research strongly suggests that there is a significant relationship between mental well-being and the functioning of the brain, and conversely, the reverse holds true in this instance as well. In light of the fact that endeavors such as speed reading promote the exploration of one's capabilities in a relaxed setting, individuals will come to recognize an enhanced sense of self-assurance when confronted with intellectual tasks, as they possess the certainty of handling them adeptly.

Assess Your Reading Rate
If you are engaged in the acquisition of speed reading skills, keeping a record of your progress will prove to be advantageous. By closely observing and measuring your reading speed during

practice sessions, you will be able to identify your progress and pinpoint any areas requiring improvement, allowing you to make the necessary adjustments. Therefore, possessing knowledge of your reading speed will prove to be advantageous.

"There exist three essential aspects that necessitate precise evaluation:

Average speed

It is of utmost importance to initially evaluate your mean velocity. This pertains to the rate of words per minute that one is capable of reading, irrespective of comprehension or memorization. To ascertain your mean velocity, select a page from a literary work and ascertain the word count per page. Utilize a timer device to accurately gauge the duration of reading a page and approximate the time required for completion. This denotes the mean velocity, commonly known as the average speed (AS), and it is conveyed in terms of words per minute.

Processing speed

An accurate estimation of reading speed necessitates the inclusion of content comprehension, which is manifested by the pace at which the information is processed. Although the primary objective of speed reading is to enhance reading speed, the ultimate purpose of reading is to attain comprehension. Hence, it is imperative that you possess both a rapid reading speed and simultaneous comprehension capabilities. Prior to assessing your level of understanding, it is essential to pose specific inquiries subsequent to gauging the mean velocity. It should be noted that the aforementioned questions must have been authored by a third party. The extent of your understanding will be ascertained based on your accuracy in answering the questions. As an illustration, if you were able to correctly answer 8 out of 14 questions, it can be inferred that your processing speed is: The postscript of the calculation is obtained by multiplying 8 by 100 and dividing the result by 14, resulting in 57%.

Memorizing speed

This represents the quantity of words one is capable of comprehending within a minute, obtained through the multiplication of one's PS by their AS, expressed in percentage form. As an illustration, in the event that you determine your average velocity to be 600 words per minute and your processing efficiency to be 75 percent, it follows that your ability to encode information into memory would be:
A calculation of 600 multiplied by 0.75 yields a total of 450 words per minute. It is evident that the goal of speed reading is to attain a significantly elevated level of speed in the process of committing information to memory. In order for this eventuality to transpire, it will be requisite for you to possess an exceedingly remarkable processing velocity, accompanied by a middling velocity on average. Once you have ascertained your reading speed, it is imperative to understand the degree of proficiency or deficiency associated with this speed.

Tools And Techniques

There exist three primary components of proficient reading:

The visual processing capabilities of your eyes

*Your level of understanding.

The cognitive faculty of your brain to comprehend the information you assimilate.

How to Enhance the Cognitive Capacity of Your Visual System

In order to develop the ability to read swiftly and efficiently, it is essential to commence by focusing on the words present within the text. Your ocular organs possess a remarkable capacity for assimilating vast amounts of information beyond your current perception. Please consider implementing the suggested strategies outlined below in order to fully exploit the capabilities of your visual system.

Refrain from fixating on each and every word, particularly those positioned at the commencement or culmination of a line.

Throughout the course of a day, employ your peripheral vision to observe objects without explicitly directing your attention towards them. This tool can be utilized for reading purposes as well. Commence the act of reading commencing from the second or third word, and conclude with the second or third word adjacent to the margin, employing your peripheral vision to encompass the words situated at the periphery.

Comprehend phrases or clusters of words

It is a common misconception that one's eyes move smoothly along a line of text; however, they actually make rapid jumps from one point to another, a phenomenon known as a saccade. The aspects that draw attention are referred to as impressions or fixations. To provide visual demonstration, kindly position the tip of a finger gently atop the closed eyelid of one eye, then proceed to carefully trace a straight trajectory with your other eye. It is advisable for you to undergo distinct and separate episodes or phases of fixation. By adopting the practice of reading in cohesive sections, it is possible to reduce the frequency of fixations per line, subsequently leading to an augmentation in reading velocity. You possess the capacity to comprehend multiple words simultaneously. Think about it. Recall the previous occasion when you were traversing the expressway and momentarily caught sight of the indications displaying "Salt Lake City" or "New York City." It is highly probable that you did not diligently peruse each and every word, but instead employed a rapid glance and were able to comprehend the intended message conveyed by the sign. With regular practice, one can enhance their words per fixation. An efficient objective is to strive for comprehending each line within just two or three fixations.

Utilize your finger, a note card, or a pen to designate your position.

Your typical visual system is inherently programmed to track and perceive movement. Therefore, the utilization of a placeholder can facilitate optimal functioning of your hardware.

To illustrate this point, employ the eye analogy previously discussed, while utilizing the index finger of your unoccupied hand to direct your movement horizontally. Instead of experiencing separate and individual movements, you will perceive a solid and coherent motion. Utilizing a digit, index card, or writing instrument as a temporary marker serves to effectively redirect the attention of one's gaze. Furthermore, it can assist in preventing the loss of your position and the need to re-read the material. Gently move your chosen instrument across and down the surface.

LESSON 6

How to Employ Strategic Reading Techniques to Achieve Expedient Outcomes with Minimal Effort

I trust that you comprehend the fact that a high reading rate serves as the fundamental prerequisite for proficient reading. Regardless of your reading speed, if you do not approach your reading materials effectively and engage with content that lacks relevance to your needs, you are squandering your time.

In order to excel in the realm of reading and learning, it is imperative to possess a deep understanding of the organizational structure of reading materials, as well as the proficiency to effectively navigate and locate desired information within them. These are the topics that will be examined in this lesson, all of which are encompassed by a concept known as...

The Strategy of Employing Various Interpretations

This is a sophisticated instrument designed to facilitate the efficient analysis of diverse materials, enabling you to promptly locate the essential information necessary for accomplishing your reading objectives. Furthermore, it serves as a means to ensure a high standard of excellence, particularly in the context of preparing for examinations and delivering presentations.

The employment of the Multiple Reading Strategy assists individuals in maintaining their motivation and concentration. It helps you concentrate and read with better comprehension. Moreover, and of utmost importance, it aids in the retention of information from the text.

Examining a passage just once, assuming that we can achieve utmost understanding and retention, is as impractical as it is foolish. Nevertheless, this is the prevailing method of instruction for the majority of us when it comes to reading. When we encounter failure in our academic pursuits and perform poorly in examinations, our teacher's response often entails the directive to 'devote more efforts to studying.' However, it remains crucial to discern the true essence of this instruction: what exactly does 'studying harder' entail? Certainly, the solution would be to carefully review the material once more.

Verbatim, Starting from the Initial Page Until the Final One.

Not good. Not good at all. It is highly probable that not only will you become increasingly disinterested in having to revisit the content, but you will also begin to encounter significant levels of psychological tension. Upcoming books and examinations are imminent, and the available time is insufficient to manage these demands.

Reading a book in its entirety is suitable for nighttime or for leisurely reading. However, when it comes to reading under time constraints with a focus on achieving optimal results, which accounts for approximately 90 percent of our reading activities, it proves to be an extraordinarily inefficient use of time. Here's why:

It has a tendency to render the act of reading a monotonous undertaking, compelling one to peruse the material in a passive, non-engaged fashion. As a consequence, concentration and comprehension issues arise.

You sift through copious amounts of extraneous material in order to isolate minute but relevant fragments of information.

You read with a lack of purpose or a diminished sense of purpose. You aimlessly traverse an expansive ocean of language. This places you in a vulnerable position, subject to the author's control.

Observing a voluminous tome spanning 1,000 pages, with the knowledge that complete perusal is obligatory, instills a sense of discouragement and diminishes motivation. It tends to cultivate a pessimistic disposition towards various forms of literature.

The magnitude of the undertaking highlights the limited availability of time. This leads to an increase in stress levels, which can have negative effects on the process of learning and retaining information.

I could continue elaborating, however, I believe you have a clear understanding of the concept.

Upon encountering the term "the Multiple Reading Strategy," one might be inclined to infer that it involves the practice of reading texts on multiple occasions.

You're right, we do.

However, doesn't this approach involve a greater investment of time compared to the traditional method of reading? In the traditional method, one simply reads a piece of material once and concludes the reading process.

Absolutely not. Indeed, when employing this particular approach correctly, one can considerably reduce their study duration by 50%. When engaging in the task of gathering information through reading, particularly within a professional business setting, it is possible to achieve a reduction in reading time of up to 80 percent. I'm not kidding. The effectiveness of the

Multiple Reading Strategy is truly unparalleled.

One could argue that, in comparison to conventional reading approaches, the Multiple Reading Strategy is...

An Elegant Approach to Engaging with Literary Resources.

When I mention that you go through a book multiple times, I am not implying that you read the entire text during each iteration. No, I am not implying that the utilization of multiple exposures is a prerequisite for the optimal effectiveness of the strategy. Occasionally, a single iteration suffices. It is contingent upon the specific objectives one has with regard to reading, and the timing and location at which such objectives are accomplished.

This exemplifies the efficacy of the Multiple Reading Strategy. You adapt it to suit your intended objectives.

What you are about to uncover holds the key to truly enhancing your reading proficiency. A resource that aids in maintaining command over all of your reading endeavors. It is anticipated that the techniques acquired in Speed Reading Secrets will result in a considerable time-saving effect, surpassing any other knowledge or skills previously acquired.

Prior to immersing ourselves and embarking on the next phase, we shall further focus on enhancing your reading speed.

Here is...

The exercise titled 'Dynamic Reading'

We shall commence by presenting the diagram pertaining to exercise 11. Please observe the content and familiarize yourself with the sequential procedures.

The activity commences by engaging in a reading exercise of new material for a duration of three minutes. Afterwards, you will engage in two iterations of reading practice. First and foremost, a brief two-minute reading session will facilitate an accelerated progression, propelling you to a speed 1.5 times faster than your initial pace. Subsequently, engage in a one-minute perusal of the identical content, allowing for a reading pace three times faster than the previous practice.

Following that, you will engage in an additional three-minute reading exercise using different materials. Subsequently, in a similar manner to our initial approach, we will embark upon a two-minute and a one-minute exercise in order to enhance reading speed.

Lastly, you will peruse the entire section with utmost celerity in order to achieve comprehensive understanding. Given that this material has already been addressed, I anticipate that you will proceed at an accelerated pace, despite your ultimate aim of achieving complete understanding.

The purpose behind reviewing the same material during the final reading is to exemplify the ease with which one can increase their speed in familiar content – a skill that will be frequently employed in the Multiple Reading Strategy.

In order to facilitate the maintenance of an appropriate pace during your reading practice, I kindly request that you make a notation of "1:00" at the midway point of each three-minute reading segment.

Therefore, during the preliminary exercise reading (which lasts for two minutes), it is important to note that when one minute has elapsed, you should ideally be at the "1:00" point.

Subsequently, for the subsequent reading exercise, you will strike through the designation "1:00" and substitute it with the notation "0:30". This is due to the requirement of reading for a duration of one minute and ensuring that the "0:30" mark has been exceeded after thirty seconds.

Additionally, as part of the effort to enhance your ability to remember and understand the material, you will engage in Recall Trees following each reading segment. This exercise encompasses the four supplementary readings.

In this exercise it will be a big help if you use one of the desktop timers I suggested in the beginning of the workbook (page xii "It's About Time"). Merely adjust the timer to audibly indicate the moment when you should reach the midpoint of each rehearsal session. For instance, in the scenario given, if your designated reading time is 1:00 and you have marked the point of "0:30" as the halfway mark within the text, you will have a precise indication of your position when the computer announces, "Thirty seconds remaining."

Please select a practice manual for the exercise: preferably one that is of lower difficulty level and does not contain excessive fragmented text and illustrations. I have previously expressed this sentiment and I reiterate it now: it is advisable to engage in the practice of augmenting one's reading speed through the utilization of less complex material, as this approach facilitates swifter advancement. However, the most remarkable aspect lies in the fact that, upon transitioning to more challenging texts for your routine reading, you will discover an instantaneously elevated reading speed.

Are you prepared for the physical activity? Proceed with enthusiasm! Additionally, it is important to remember to unwind and consistently...

Make Your Mark!

Exercise 11 is a task focused on dynamic reading techniques and involves gathering information from a given passage.

Objective: Engage in active reading with a adaptable reading pace. Enhance the rate of reading and grasp of content.

Required materials for this activity include a book of your preference, a timing device, a recall sheet, and a writing utensil.

Instructions:

1. Please proceed to your designated starting point, Mark A. Please engage in a 3-minute reading session and indicate the concluding point as B. Do a recall. Compute your reading rate. At the midpoint of this section, record the time as 1:00.

2. Please engage in the exercise of reading the identical section within a time span of 2 minutes. Ensure that you have surpassed the one-minute threshold by the time the clock reaches 1:00, or alternatively, increase your pace to reach the designated endpoint in a timely manner. Please recollect any information that you can about your

family tree. Please delete the time 1:00 and replace it with 0:30. Speed = 1.5x

3. Please engage in the activity of reading the identical passage within a time frame of 60 seconds for the purpose of improving your skills. Ensure that you surpass the 0:30 threshold within a duration of less than 30 seconds, or alternatively, accelerate in order to reach your final point. Retrieve any remaining words in your memory that are lingering on your recall tree. Speed = 3x

4. Please browse through the contents of B for a duration of 3 minutes. Please designate the concluded location as point C. Do a recall. Compute your reading rate. Please record the time as 1:00 when you reach the midpoint of the section that you have just read.

5. Engage in the exercise of reading the identical passage within a duration of

120 seconds. Exceed the 1:00 mark within a duration of less than 1 minute or increase your pace to achieve your end goal. Please endeavor to recollect any information pertaining to your lineage. Please strike through the entry for 1:00 and substitute it with 0:30. Speed = 1.5x

6. Please engage in the exercise of reading the identical passage within a timeframe of 60 seconds. Exceed the 30-second mark before reaching the 0:30 mark, or alternatively, accelerate in order to meet your final deadline. Recall anything you can. Speed = 3x

7. Efficiently peruse the content between A and C while maintaining a strong grasp of the material. Given that you have already familiarized yourself with this content, endeavor to proceed at an accelerated pace compared to your usual speed. Please include any additional

information you can recall on your mnemonic diagram. Compute your rate.

Please be advised: The preceding observation illustrates the consistent possibility of achieving greater speed when engaging with familiar or less significant content, or that which is comparatively easier.

Please document the findings obtained from the readings undertaken at positions 1, 4, and 7 within your Progress Profile, located at the commencement of the workbook.

Very well, we have successfully completed the exercise. Now, let us redirect our attention to the Multiple Reading Strategy. The primary topic of our discussion will be...

Getting Organized

Having established a foundation for our reading speed and being prepared to acquire further skills, it is advisable to ensure that you are adequately organized in order to maximize the benefits of speed reading. If you don\'t do a bit of preliminary work, make sure that your lighting makes reading easier and that you are free of distractions before you even get started. Preparation in advance holds nearly identical importance to the act of speed reading itself; therefore, we will dedicate some time to delve deeper into this aspect.

If one simply selects the initial available option, assumes a seated position in a dimly lit area, and engages in conversing with others whilst attempting to enhance speed reading skills, the outcome is likely to be unsatisfactory.

You will discover that you are unable to read at the desired pace and that you fail to retain the contents of the document. Fortunately, through effective organization and implementation of the strategies outlined in this chapter, you will be able to create an optimal setting and devise an appropriate plan to achieve success in the practice of speed reading.

Arrange your reading material in order of importance and develop a systematic approach.

Prior to commencing, it is imperative to review our allocated reading materials and ascertain which components hold the utmost significance for your individual undertaking. It is highly probable that you will need to allocate time towards perusing various forms of literature, while also prioritizing the completion of paramount tasks. Do you possess a specific document that requires completion? Do you have a specific sequence in which you prefer tasks to be completed? Organize your reading materials and tasks based on your preferred sequence. If it becomes necessary to engage in activities involving these materials, such as the generation of a research-based report, it is advisable to compile all the relevant data and ensure that the required items are readily accessible within a centralized location. It is surprising how allocating a brief period at the outset to establish priorities for your tasks can significantly enhance efficiency and time management over the course of time.

You fundamentally need to utilize this section in order to formulate a formidable strategy that will facilitate your initial progress. It is advised to prioritize the tasks that require your attention, determine the allocated time frame for their completion, and identify the comprehensive scope of each task. Additionally, you may devise a comprehensive schedule outlining the approach you will adopt to effectively complete the reading requirements for each document, thereby ensuring optimal time management.

Commence by employing the hierarchical system.

In this section, we shall allocate some time to acquaint ourselves with the foundational concepts by perusing the material and gaining an understanding of its contents prior to commencing the reading. Lacking prior knowledge of the material you are about to read can significantly impede your pace and comprehension. By employing this approach, one can acquire a preliminary overview of the forthcoming content, thereby expediting the reading process by obviating the need for subsequent catching up.

Firstly, we shall commence by examining the accompanying document's table of contents. If executed proficiently, one can derive insights regarding the subjects to be addressed within the document by analyzing the chapter titles and subheadings present within the table of contents. Please review this material and acquaint yourself with the subjects discussed therein.

Subsequently, we will proceed with an examination of the introduction and conclusion sections of our document in order to identify the pivotal elements contained within. If the report is prepared in a competent manner, it will furnish you with valuable insights pertaining to the subjects encompassed within the entirety of the document, thereby expediting the process. Please allocate a period of time for carefully perusing the aforementioned materials and subsequently ascertain whether there are any inquiries posed towards the termination of the document or chapter, akin to those commonly found in textbooks. These inquiries will serve to facilitate your understanding of the most crucial subjects as well.

Lastly, it is advisable to dedicate time to thoroughly perusing the opening and closing paragraphs contained within each of the divided sections, if applicable, of the document. These documents serve as concise overviews of each section, offering valuable assistance. There is no need to invest a significant amount of time poring over this material. Please peruse a few pages to acquire fundamental knowledge.

Presently, it is appropriate to commence with the practice of speed reading. It is expected that you possess a comprehensive understanding of the document's contents, reducing the necessity to read every word in entirety. Instead, focus on identifying the salient aspects of the section. You will have the opportunity to employ a range of speed reading techniques, including the method of chunking, which will be comprehensively discussed in later chapters of this book. By doing so, you can efficiently read through the document, accomplishing the task within a matter of minutes as opposed to dedicating several hours to it. Establishing the hierarchical system may require some time, however, you will discover that it facilitates access to critical information, particularly in the initial stages, and subsequently enables efficient comprehension and expeditious navigation of the document.

Strategies and techniques for creating an optimal setting for the practice of speed reading

It is crucial to ensure you are situated in an optimal environment prior to commencing the practice of speed reading. In the event of suboptimal posture, numerous distractions in the vicinity, or inadequate lighting conditions, the initiation of speed reading will prove to be exceedingly challenging. Here are several suggestions that can assist you in establishing an optimal environment for speed reading:

- Select a location with adequate illumination: Lighting plays a crucial role in the initial stages of engaging in speed reading. In what manner can one be expected to decipher the textual content on a given page, let alone comprehend it with swiftness, if their visual perception is compromised? Ensure that the ambiance of the room is offering satisfactory illumination. The inclusion of a reading lamp can facilitate improved visibility of the page, thereby mitigating potential ocular strain over an extended period of time.

• Minimize distractions: When engaged in speed reading, it is vital to minimize any potential distractions. This implies that you should switch off the excessively loud music, ensure that you are positioned away from the television, and strictly prohibit any interruptions or distractions from entering the room while you attend to this task. These diversions will render it exceedingly difficult to focus on the text before you, thereby restricting both your pace and your understanding.

• Enable soft instrumental melodies: Certain individuals may encounter difficulty focusing on reading in a completely silent environment.

Individuals might continue enunciating the words they perceive internally or be subject to auditory distractions, like the sound of a passing vehicle or other noises, impeding their ability to maintain focus on speed reading. Certain types of quiet music, particularly classical music, can prove most beneficial as it provides a soothing melodic backdrop and has been demonstrated to enhance concentration levels.

- Maintain an upright posture: The way you hold your body is significant in the context of speed reading. When assuming a slouched posture, you inadvertently create the perception of relaxation, which subsequently hampers your ability to concentrate effectively on the task at hand. It is imperative to ensure that you maintain an upright seated position, as adopting a proper posture significantly enhances your ability to concentrate on the assigned task.

• Ensure comfort: While maintaining proper posture is crucial for enhancing focus and productivity, it is equally important to ensure your overall comfort. If you experience discomfort or physical discomfort or encounter any other form of physical impairment while seated, your attention will be drawn towards addressing the issue at hand rather than focusing on the content of your reading material. Discover a suitable location that promotes proper posture and enables optimal comfort.

• Consume a modest amount of food prior to commencing: In the event of hunger, it is advisable to partake in a light snack prior to initiating the practice of speed reading. If you experience hunger pangs in your stomach, it is highly likely that you will encounter difficulties in comprehending the material presented before you. Ensure that it is merely a modest refreshment, striking a balance between satiation and excess without inducing a feeling of overindulgence. Having a satiated stomach is equally detrimental to concentration as having an empty stomach.

• Procure a beverage: Considering the duration of your speed reading endeavors, it is plausible that you may experience some degree of thirst throughout the activity. Should you allocate an excessive amount of time pondering over the act of quenching your thirst or fixating on your need for a beverage, it is imperative to acknowledge that you risk overlooking pertinent information present in the text before you. Moreover, your reading pace may decelerate as a consequence. Please bring a glass of water to ensure that should you become thirsty, you can readily hydrate without unnecessary interruption to your work.

It is crucial to establish organization before embarking on the journey of speed reading. If one lacks adequate preparedness and readiness to engage in speed reading, it is likely to result in encountering numerous challenges throughout the process and potentially hinder the necessary level of concentration required for success. Ensure that you utilize these tools, and undoubtedly, you shall commence your speed reading journey, augmenting your words per minute with remarkable swiftness.

Speed reading, also known as rapid reading, is a technique that enables individuals to efficiently consume written materials such as books, articles, and textual content with increased celerity. Possessing such a skill is highly beneficial, particularly in our contemporary era which presents numerous opportunities for acquiring knowledge. Various techniques exist for enhancing reading speed, and we will delve deeper into their nuances promptly.

Typically, individuals reading at an "ordinary" pace exhibit a comprehension level of around 60%. For individuals who attempt the practice of speed reading without employing appropriate techniques, the efficacy of the process is noticeably diminished, resulting in a reduction of approximately 50%. This implies that the act of reading hastily directly undermines your level of understanding, thereby offering limited long-term benefits. If one fails to grasp the content being read, it will pose a significant obstacle to the process of studying or acquiring the necessary knowledge.

Fortunately, authentic speed reading is also accompanied by a high level of comprehension. Not only will you acquire the ability to read at an accelerated pace, but you will also enhance your comprehension and assimilation of the material. While there are some reading experts who hold the belief that speed reading does not yield optimal efficiency as it adversely affects comprehension levels, there exists a significant group of proponents of speed reading who vehemently disagree with this assertion. Indeed, they are of the opinion that the practice of speed reading has the potential to enhance both one's memory retention and cognitive intelligence. One plausible explanation for the limited effectiveness of speed reading among many individuals could be attributed to their failure in acquiring the skill through appropriate techniques.

In order to acquire efficient speed reading skills, it is imperative to first dismantle or relinquish certain established reading patterns. This will facilitate the development of your ability to read at a faster pace while ensuring that your comprehension remains at a consistently high level. This represents the authentic interpretation of speed reading. This is the objective one should strive for in order to truly attain mastery in the skill of speed-reading.

Unveiling the Facts of Speed Reading

For an extended period, speed reading has been advocated by experts as a desirable skill for the general public. In recent times, a number of applications have emerged purporting to facilitate instantaneous speed reading. Regrettably, these purported "experts" and applications do not truly deliver all that they claim to offer. Consequently, can it be inferred that speed reading is merely a fallacy? Certainly not! It is indeed a genuine aptitude that can be acquired through the acquisition of accurate knowledge and diligent training.

The majority of individuals possess the ability to peruse written content within the range of 200 to 400 words per minute. The most proficient speed readers assert that they have the capability to read at a pace ranging from 1,000 to 1,700 words per minute. This figure is considerably higher when juxtaposed with the typical reading speed of an average individual. These claims aren\\\'t baseless. The professionals possess the capability to engage in expedient reading without compromising their ability to comprehend and retain the content. In order to achieve this, they have implemented certain established techniques for speed-reading, which will be elaborated upon in the subsequent sections.

These strategies facilitate the eradication of ingrained and enduring poor reading practices that have been acquired in the past and consistently employed throughout one's lifetime. While it may appear to be an arduous and unattainable endeavor, the truth is that it is within reach. Allow us to consider one of the most prevalent instances as illustration in order to enhance your comprehension of this concept. Speed reading eliminates the need for extensive cognitive engagement in deciphering unfamiliar and intricate concepts, rendering the act of reading a notably mechanized undertaking.

Typically, within this particular procedure, one would engage in the act of "fixation" to examine a single word or a cluster of words. On average, the duration spent for this examination is approximately 0.25 seconds, following which the eyes are redirected to the subsequent words which, on average, require about 0.1 seconds. Upon performing this task on one or two occasions, it is advisable to allocate a brief period of time to comprehend the word or phrase recently encountered in the estimated time range of 0.3 to 0.5 seconds. The cumulative effect of these fixations and pauses contributes to the limitation faced by individuals reading at a typical pace, capping their reading speed at approximately 200 - 400 words per minute. In the case of proficient readers, they possess the ability to minimize the frequency of fixations and interruptions during the process of reading.

This serves as a singular instance illustrating the methods by which one may enhance their reading speed by reversing the ingrained reading habits accrued during one's developmental years. Subsequently, as you familiarize yourself with additional speed-reading techniques, you gradually acquire new practices that facilitate enhanced reading speed. Undoubtedly, it can be observed that speed reading is an attainable skill. It is imperative that everyone acquires this fundamental skill at the earliest opportunity.

What are the Advantages of Acquiring Speed Reading Skills?

In our contemporary society characterized by rapidity, the ability to engage in rapid reading has emerged as a fundamental proficiency. It will facilitate the rapid assimilation and efficient processing of substantial volumes of information. Moreover, this will facilitate your focus on the remaining tasks. Presented below are several compelling justifications for acquiring the skill of speed reading:

To enhance both your concentration abilities and your aptitude for comprehending written material.

To augment your capacity to retain all the information you peruse.

To assist you in overcoming any challenges in learning, thereby facilitating a smoother learning experience for you.

To greatly enhance the pace at which you read.

To gain insight into the synergistic functioning of the ocular and cerebral faculties in assimilating and retaining an extensive range of textual data.

To increase your vocabulary.

In order to optimize your time efficiency and foster your reading proficiency,

To enhance one's capacity for assimilating a significantly greater volume of written content.

Whilst the concept of acquiring speed reading skills may seem daunting to certain individuals, in actuality, it is not. Similar to acquiring any valuable new skill, the greater your understanding and commitment to speed reading, the more effortless it will become for you. Through consistent practice, you will be providing relief to your eyes as they won't be subjected to excessive physical exertion. The innate cadence and tempo of accelerated reading facilitate enhanced comprehension of the presented information. This is due to the fact that there is no need for frequent interruptions in order to revisit previously read material for comprehension purposes. This phenomenon results in a loss of concentration and generates feelings of boredom if the content being read fails to captivate your interest. In the end, irrespective of the frequency of your perusals, you will fail to retain the information contained within the text.

The Concept Of Achieving A 300% Increase In Reading Speed Within A Span Of Merely Six Hours

To what extent would your productivity increase if you were able to accomplish your mandatory reading in only one-third of the typical timeframe? One can merely conceive the myriad possibilities and potentials that could arise.

To enhance your rate of comprehension, it merely entails developing mastery of your intricate motor coordination. Implemented trials aimed at enhancing human reading speed within a specified timeframe have yielded notable advancements, with average improvements surpassing an impressive 300% and beyond. The foundation of such experiments is grounded in the principles that define the human visual system. By gaining a comprehensive understanding of the system's functioning, we could potentially eliminate our inefficiencies and enhance our capacity for rapid reading (while simultaneously improving information retention).

The strategy involves reducing the number and duration of fixations per line in order to encourage faster-than-average reading. Here, we are presented with the concept of engaging in the act of reading by employing a series of saccadic movements, as opposed to the conventional method of reading in linear fashion. Every saccade concludes with a fixation, often referred to as a momentary snapshot encompassing all the words located within the attended region. To untrained participants, the fixation would need to endure for a duration of either a quarter or half a second. You can personally demonstrate this phenomenon by closing one eye and gently positioning a fingertip just above the closed eyelid. Subsequently, you proceed to carefully examine the material in a linear progression, utilizing your alternate eye. Through the process outlined, you will uncover individual and unique motions characterized by intermittent periods of fixation.

The revelation (regarding the capacity to achieve a 300% increase in reading speed within a mere 6-hour timeframe) is supplemented by valuable speed-reading strategies, which involve the elimination of back-skipping and regression. It is contingent upon our capacity to employ conditioning exercises that facilitate the development of our horizontal peripheral vision span, particularly enhancing the number of words that are processed during each fixation. Before we can commence evaluating our speed-reading abilities, it is imperative that we condition ourselves to meet the demands and specifications of the established and verified technique. This conditioning process involves honing our reading skills to perform at a speed approximately three times faster than our intended reading rate, while also ensuring comprehension of the material.

You commence the process by establishing your baseline, which corresponds to your presently achieved reading speed. This objective is attained through the process of calculating the number of words contained within a specified set of five lines from a literary work. To obtain the average number of words per line, divide the result by 5. Subsequently, ascertain the mean number of lines per page by tallying the number of text lines featured on five distinct pages. Subsequently, perform a division of the obtained outcome by a factor of 5, followed by multiplication with the mean number of words per line. What you presently possess is the customary ratio of words to pages.

Utilize a timer to engage in a 1-minute comprehensive reading of your material. Engage in reading and achieve comprehension – read at your typical pace. Subsequently, ascertain the quantification of lines encompassing each of your words on an average, and subsequently calculate your rate of words per minute.

As previously stated, eliminating regression and back-skipping constitutes a crucial element of speed-reading. Now that this matter has been resolved, you can direct your attention towards the ensuing stage of your transition in speed-reading - perceptual expansion. When focusing your gaze on the middle of a computer screen, you will observe that you can effectively perceive and process the surrounding edges. Developing and enhancing your ability to recognize and capture information using your peripheral vision will significantly bolster your reading speed, potentially even resulting in a threefold increase or more.

After acquiring proficiency in this task, you will be able to calculate your revised word-per-minute reading pace. Please peruse the text for a duration of 60 seconds, reading at a rapid pace while maintaining comprehension. Calculate the number of lines obtained and multiply it by your prior average words-per-line to ascertain your updated words-per-minute ratio.

READING FAST FROM SCREEN

In our preceding lessons, it has been emphasized that, in order to adapt your reading speed, you should adopt a linear approach to read the introduction, conclusion, and Tolmach sentences, while applying a different method for reading the remaining parts of the text. Right. In essence, your initial step involves previewing the text by gradually reading the introduction and conclusion in order to gain an understanding of its content. In the second phase, one ought to peruse the headings and topic sentences, whereas the third stage primarily entails active engagement in the reading process. This process is referred to as a multi-step reading procedure, which comprises three distinct stages: pre-viewing, providing an overview, and finally, reading. What is the utility/benefit of being aware of this? Many individuals read at a slow pace because they lack prior knowledge about the content they are reading. Therefore, it is imperative for individuals to exercise meticulousness in order to enhance their reading speed. Through the utilization of this multi-step reading process, individuals can ascertain the anticipated functionalities of the technology, thereby enabling them to surpass the reading speed of an average individual. One of the contributing factors to individuals' slow reading speed is their tendency to read on a per-word basis. One can enhance their reading pace by acquiring the ability to process multiple words simultaneously. This project pertains to the third phase of our reading process, which is known as the read stage. Essentially, what I am suggesting is that rather than reading each individual word, it is beneficial to focus on reading groups of words. This is a common practice in our daily lives. In any case, as an illustration, when encountering a roadside banner advertisement, we devote our attention to comprehending the entire message being conveyed. Right. Therefore, employing an analogous approach to that utilized for other sections, one can effectively apply this method of grouping words. It is recommended to categorize each line within the passage into three distinct sections: the introduction, the body, and the conclusion. Essentially, you are focusing your gaze on a line at three distinct positions: the starting point, the midpoint, and the endpoint. Your task here is to concentrate on three to four words for each fixation point. This may prove to be a formidable task for novice individuals; however, with consistent dedication and ample practice, one can acquire a proficient command over this specific technique. Try it right now. Proceed by segmenting every line of the given text into three distinct points. Attempt to engage in text examination utilizing the fixation technique for a duration of one minute. You have the option to temporarily halt this video for a duration of one minute. Good luck. So, how did the situation unfold? Have you successfully identified and articulated three key points? It is imperative for each and every one of us to possess the capacity to read with proficiency, correct? Effective interpersonal communication is indispensable for establishing positive connections and attaining desired outcomes. The concept of speed reading originated from this notion, wherein individuals can process significant amounts of information by reading at an average pace. However, with the ability to engage in speed reading, one can further enhance their reading efficiency and accomplish a greater volume of tasks within a shorter timeframe.

MULTIPLE READING PROCESS

One challenge associated with the acquisition of speed reading abilities is that, oftentimes, one completes a book before realizing its lack of interest. Quote by Franklin P. Jones, were you aware that the current world record holder in speed reading boasts the impressive ability to effortlessly read at a rate of four thousand seven hundred words per minute? This signifies that an individual can effortlessly navigate lengthy novels and books within a time frame of under an hour. Nevertheless, at such a rapid pace, there is scarcely anything remaining to acquire and retain. If you happen to be reading Inferno or Harry Potter, it is acceptable to engage in swift reading, considering the primary objective is amusement. Nevertheless, in the context of exam preparation, it is necessary to cultivate a mentality of curiosity and receptivity to acquire a comprehensive understanding of the textual information. Reading it alone will not suffice for you to acquire knowledge. Today, I would like to address the topic of memory as it pertains to reading. Basically retention. There are, in fact, three methods to retain information from what you have read. It is advisable to engage in the training of one's cognitive abilities through techniques such as impression Association and repetition. An excellent point of origin for grasping the concept of book retention lies in comprehending several fundamental methods by which our brain encodes and retains information. Presented herewith are three distinct factors worthy of consideration. First impression, secondly. Association number 3. Repetition. Suppose for instance that you have perused Dale Carnegie's renowned work, How to Win Friends and Influence People. You deeply appreciated the information and sought to retain it to the fullest extent. Allow me to present the method for accomplishing that task. Start with impression. Allow yourself to be captivated by the written content and envision a vivid scenario in your imagination. Moreover, one could further enhance the impact by incorporating elements of grandeur, surprise, or even a personal cameo appearance. If Dale Carnegie is elucidating his aversion towards criticism. Envision a scenario in which you are bestowed with the esteemed Nobel Prize for Peace, only to exhibit an unconventional display of celebration by forcefully dropping the prestigious award. Onto the days. An alternative suggestion is to embark on another excursion of impact, which involves vocalizing a significant passage. It is worth noting that, for certain individuals, auditory stimuli may evoke a heightened sensitivity to information compared to visual cues. The following step involves establishing an association between the text and existing knowledge. This methodology is employed with utmost efficacy in the realms of memorization and the establishment of memory palaces. If, concerning Carnegie's book, there is a specific example that you wish to preserve. Reflect upon a past occurrence in which you were involved in a particular instance with the principal. Building associations through prior knowledge is an excellent approach. And lastly repetition. The greater the frequency of repetition, the stronger the likelihood of retention. This phenomenon can be achieved by perusing a specific passage verbatim, or by selectively emphasizing and transcribing it. Subsequently revisiting and consistently applying these three mnemonic techniques will facilitate your gradual improvement over time, as your diligent practice will lead to enhanced memorization capacity.

What Does Speed-Reading Entail?

Put concisely, speed-reading entails the practice of reading at an accelerated pace relative to one's usual speed, employing strategic techniques such as controlled eye movements and efficient skimming, all while ensuring satisfactory comprehension.

When indulging in the act of reading, one actively stimulates and involves several cognitive faculties including the brain, mouth, ears, and eyes. When engaging in speed-reading, there is a significant increase in the activation of these cerebral regions. Speed-reading involves the following:

Sight

The initial characteristic of speed-reading entails the manner in which the reader perceives the words being read. The study carried out during the 1920s demonstrated that individuals have the capacity to read only one word at a time. The findings indicated that the act of reading entails a visual process wherein the reader's eyes traverse horizontally across the page, sequentially apprehending each word. Based on the findings of this study, individuals categorized as fast readers demonstrated a heightened ability to rapidly identify and comprehend written words.

In contrast to the aforementioned research, recent discoveries indicate that individuals who engage in consistent reading possess the capacity to perceive and comprehend not only isolated words, but also multiple words simultaneously. As one's gaze traverses a written page, one is capable of comprehending approximately one to five words simultaneously through swift glances. However, with speed-reading:

Unless you come across unfamiliar words, you will be able to process multiple words at once when reading.

* By broadening your visual perspective, you will enhance your ability to effortlessly comprehend multiple words within a single glance.

Once your visual scope broadens, you will acquire the capacity to peruse any page both horizontally and vertically.

Additionally, you will acquire the aptitude to comprehend and interpret words across two or even three lines within a provided text.

Reading silently

Typically, during the process of reading, individuals commonly engage in inner speech, silently pronouncing the words in their mind. This phenomenon occurs as a result of your familiarity with employing the auditory approach to reading. In educational institutions, educators commonly instruct young learners to decode words by phonetically pronouncing the individual letters and their combinations. This valuable ability proves beneficial for children at the early stages of reading proficiency.

The sole issue associated with this methodology is that it hinders the pace of your reading. One finds themselves reading at the pace of their speech rather than that of their cognitive processing. The act of silently articulating words mentally corresponds to an augmented duration of reading. In the practice of speed reading, the process of audibly articulating words in one's mind is referred to as vocalization.

In order to acquire the skill of speed-reading, it is advisable to develop the ability to refrain from vocalizing while engaging in the act of reading.

Comprehending

The primary objective of engaging in reading is to achieve a comprehensive understanding of the material being read. The degree to which you grasp the material, your familiarity with the subject matter, and the extent of your lexicon all hinge on your reading velocity.

By engaging in rapid reading, you enhance your comprehension skills as you process multiple words simultaneously, thereby solidifying your ability to grasp their intended meaning. When engaging in rapid reading techniques, you concurrently enhance your breadth of knowledge and expand your lexicon.

Concentration

Every form of reading necessitates focus, even if that focus is ephemeral. Nevertheless, in the practice of speed-reading, one must exert deliberate and unwavering focus, as it entails performing several simultaneous activities.

In order to engage in efficient speed reading, it is imperative to engage in the process of visually perceiving and comprehending the written words on a page, remain highly attentive to the primary concepts conveyed by the writer, cultivate a mental framework akin to that of the author, and approach the text from a vantage point that discerns the minutiae from the substantively significant content. Consequently, this implies that it is necessary to acquire the skill of discerning when to engage in rapid reading, skim through content, and when to adopt a slower pace in order to grasp the fundamental essence of the material.

Prior to delving deeper into the concept of speed-reading, it is paramount to acquire an understanding of the various categorizations of reading.

Chapter Three: Enhancing Reading Speed

Speed reading entails the rapid comprehension and assimilation of entire phrases or sentences in a cohesive manner, as opposed to the mere identification of individual words.

The volume of information we contend with appears to be expanding on a daily basis, whether it pertains to the abundance of electronic correspondence, work-related documents, and online platforms, or the influx of social media content, literary resources, and printed publications in our personal lives. It is probable that we experience a sense of urgency to process this information at a faster pace, in order to remain updated and ensure our ability to make well-informed decisions.

The majority of individuals possess the ability to read at a standard pace of 250 words per minute (wpm), although certain individuals exhibit a natural propensity for reading at a faster rate. However, possessing the skill of rapid reading could potentially result in a twofold increase of this rate.

Speed reading encompasses the subsequent abilities:

Observation: The act of scanning or perceiving is considered the paramount skill in the practice of speed reading. This entails acquiring the skill to identify pertinent terms within a text rather than comprehensively reading every individual word within a sentence.

Perusal: Focus your attention solely on the pertinent sentence within a given paragraph, particularly when you possess prior knowledge about the subject matter. Cease your vocalization while you are engaged in the act of reading. Vocalizing slows you down.

Understanding: The act of reading encompasses understanding, and with the practice of speed reading, your capacity to comprehend expands significantly as you process and comprehend multiple words simultaneously.

Focusing: The ability to concentrate is paramount when it comes to speed reading. It necessitates an unwavering focus due to the simultaneous engagement with multiple actions, such as perceiving the words, identifying crucial terms, comprehending the concepts conveyed within the written content, and so forth.

Barriers To Speed Reading

Nowadays, the abundance of reading material surpasses our wildest expectations from half a century ago. Each passing day, a relentless influx of new material becomes available, leaving us pondering whether it will ever be possible to fully peruse and comprehend the entirety of it. Although it may be impractical to read all of them within the span of one lifetime, we can aspire to read all of our beloved selections by acquiring proficiency in the art of speed reading. The typical reading rate ranges between 200 and 400 words per minute. Speed readers are capable of reading at significantly elevated rates. According to theoretical principles, an individual has the ability to read at the pace of their own thoughts. There exist individuals who assert that they are capable of reading at a rate of 25,000 words per minute!

Extensive study and research have been conducted in order to ascertain the factors that contribute to individuals' ability to read at an accelerated pace. Speed reading entails the integration of diverse strategies that facilitate accelerated reading. There exist several factors that prevent individuals from reading at a pace surpassing a specific threshold. The primary factor is that individuals have a tendency to vocalize while reading. The rate at which speech may be conveyed is approximately 400 words per minute, and if one happens to be reading aloud, their reading pace is contingent upon their delivery speed. To enhance your reading speed, it is necessary to first abstain from this habitual behavior.

The concept of sub-vocalization is acquired during the early stages of literacy development in childhood. The most effective approach to eradicating this habit is to be mindful of it during the act of reading. Make a conscious endeavor to refrain from speaking the words audibly. The term "aloud" in this context does not exclusively connote the literal act of speaking audibly; rather, it may encompass the concept of mentally articulating the words while silently reading. This can also have a detrimental impact on the rate at which the text is being read.

Develop the ability to read at the same speed as your thoughts. The act of reading should be akin to observing a video wherein word duplication does not occur. You simply perceive and comprehend the intended message conveyed by the video. The act of reading should involve perceiving and comprehending rather than merely listening to and comprehending the words. It will require a considerable investment of time and effort on your part to completely eradicate this habit. However, once you have successfully cultivated the practice of absorbing information through visual perception, your reading velocity will undergo a remarkable surge.

Revisiting previously read material is another behavior that impedes the pace of your reading. Frequently, we have a tendency to revisit previously read texts. This may be attributed to a restricted lexicon or diminished focus. Please endeavor to refrain from repeatedly perusing the text. One's lexicon will gradually expand as they engage in a greater volume of reading materials. To enhance focus, commence by engaging in reading within a secluded environment. Gradually enhance your ability to concentrate by leveraging assistive devices such as an earplug. As you engage in the act of reading, your focus will naturally enhance. It is not invariably essential to peruse every word in order to comprehend the significance of the sentence. There will be specific keywords that will effectively communicate the entire meaning.

The mastery of speed reading techniques can be achieved through consistent practice and self-discipline, as they are inherently uncomplicated.

Comparing Speed Reading And Active Reading

Speed-reading is described as the alleged capacity to comprehend and process a staggering range of 10,000 to 25,000 words in a single minute. Evidently, it is not feasible to meticulously read every single word of the text using this approach. While engaging in accelerated studies, it is one matter to ascertain the denotative interpretations of lexical entities, but another matter entirely to profoundly grasp the contextual nuances within which said entities are conveyed.

Speed-reading techniques serve a purpose when:

You desire or have a necessity to peruse expediently through a written document in order to grasp its essence. Employ this methodology when you solely require a superficial understanding of a given topic. Please peruse the table of contents, headings, introductions, and summaries.

If you require a moderate degree of specificity regarding a particular subject, you would peruse the text. This process entails swiftly perusing each line while searching for the intended text, directing one's attention to the middle of the page, moving the eyes expeditiously along the page without going back. I would suggest thoroughly reviewing the chapter introductions and summaries. This approach will assist you in efficiently perusing the contents of the chapters, identifying and comprehending pivotal language and concepts.

The efficacy of speed-reading largely relies on the reader's ability to swiftly comprehend the meanings conveyed by the words present on the page. This requires the readers to have a high command of the language and the ability to differentiate between the meanings of same or similar words.

However, it is important to emphasize once again that a more deliberate and methodical approach to reading, one that involves careful analysis and critical thinking, is often necessary. The rate at which you engage in reading for various objectives possesses the potential for augmentation; however, in order to thrive in the realm of academia, the key lies in discerning when to accelerate and decelerate.

Active Reading entails cultivating a heightened level of engagement with the material being read. One of the utmost crucial facets of engaged reading is the preservation of information. Outlined below are several tactics that can be employed in order to enhance active reading skills:

Set realistic goals

Establish a reasonable timeline for each reading assignment.

Take, for instance, the decision to allocate a predetermined duration or a specific quantity of pages for reading purposes.

Do not exceed your capacity to concentrate while reading. It is of no significance if your attention span is limited—simply adjust your tasks accordingly.

Be a 'Choosy' reader

Determine the readings that are essential for your study objectives and those that are recommended but not obligatory. There may arise instances where you will be required to thoroughly peruse a complete article or chapter. On different occasions, you might seek particular information pertaining to a subject of an assignment, wherein a few pages or even a few paragraphs from a text would prove invaluable. Upon identifying the pertinent sections of a text, it may render the remaining content unnecessary to peruse. The ability to select texts enables readers to enhance their proficiency in time management.

Highlight

While thoroughly going through a document or book, it would be advantageous to make use of underlining significant points, highlighting relevant information, and utilizing the margins to include personal annotations or raise inquiries.

Direct your attention to the specific inquiry at hand.

Always approach reading with a clear set of inquiries intended to be addressed by the text. Contemplate the information you must seek. Deliberate upon the inquiries you wish to address; proactively seek out relevant responses and substantiating evidence. In order to ensure better information retention, it is imperative to adopt an inquisitive mindset and systematically query the text on the specific details you seek, thereby locating the corresponding answers within the content.

Jot down observations and record information

There exists a distinction between the two. The act of note-taking during the process of reading generally entails reproducing fragments of the text or writing down essential keywords derived directly from the passage.

To gain a comprehensive grasp of the subject matter, it is important to bear in mind that effective reading strategies are inherently connected to proficient note-taking abilities. Note-taking evolves into a heightened engagement, as one must discern and prioritize pertinent and significant information before delineating it in their own phrasing. This is an excellent approach to retaining and recalling information at a later point in time.

Use Mind-mapping techniques

Mind Maps are graphical depictions of data that individuals must highlight and preserve for subsequent utilization. It exhibits a greater level of compactness as compared to traditional notes. Mind Mapping facilitates the process of decomposing extensive projects or subjects into more manageable segments, thereby enabling effective planning without succumbing to feelings of being overwhelmed. Additionally, it proves beneficial in situations where individuals require the amalgamation of data gathered from various research sources.

An effective Mind Map visually portrays the structure of the topic, the relative significance of each point, and the interconnections among the facts. This implies their rapidity in review as information can be promptly refreshed with a cursory glance. When crafted with a palette of hues and accompanied by visual elements or illustrations, a Mind Map can even bear semblance to an artistic endeavor.

Maintain a record of your reading

It is imperative to consistently acknowledge the sources of information and ideas. Ensure that you meticulously document pertinent information such as the author's name, title of the work, place of publication, publisher, and the publication date to facilitate future retrieval of the text as needed.

When perusing a document or literary work, one may effortlessly embrace the author's framework of reasoning. This implies that there is a possibility that you might overlook the omission of crucial information or the inclusion of insignificant details. A viable approach to address this situation is to predefine a table of contents prior to commencing the reading process. Please consider which sections or subjects you anticipate encountering in this document, as well as the inquiries you desire to be addressed upon concluding the text.

When utilizing a book from the library for studying purposes, it is advisable to employ Post-It notes to meticulously document pertinent details. Ensure that page numbers are consistently recorded alongside any notes that are taken. If one is engaged in the extensive perusal of intricate technical content, it could prove advantageous to utilize or construct a compendium of specialized terms and definitions. Please ensure that you have this document within reach while reading.

Numerous accomplished students utilize a combination of strategies comprising of highlighting, taking notes in a distinct binder, and summarizing after intervals in the text. In order to guarantee your success, it is imperative to establish a framework that enables efficient retrieval of specific types of information.

In conclusion, for the purpose of enhancing reading efficiency, it is advisable to discern the specific knowledge one aims to acquire from the material and employ proactive reading techniques to facilitate comprehension. The acquisition of adept reading skills necessitates consistent practice and dedication. The utilization of these strategies will lead to an increased level of success.

• Chapter 2: Various Approaches to Speed Reading

The initial methodology we shall discuss is Meta-guiding. This technique entails the act of utilizing a digit or an instrument, such as a writing implement, namely a pen or a pencil, to direct and expedite the movement of one's gaze along the entirety of a written passage. I have observed that you were not traversing the entire width of the page or engaging in horizontal eye movements. You are perusing the entirety of the page, by commencing your gaze from the uppermost section and gradually scanning it to the lowermost part. This is the technique which Evelyn Wood initially commenced to develop. This methodology entails delineating imperceptible shapes on a specific page of text in order to enhance the reader's visual range for the purpose of expedited reading. To put it differently, you are not merely increasing the pace at which you read horizontally, but rather employing your peripheral vision in conjunction with central fixation to efficiently process all the words within your visual field.

This methodology endeavors to mitigate the concept of subvocalization, which manifests when individuals silently articulate the words in their mind. As an illustration, in the event that you have ever engaged in the act of perusing a literary work and rather than visualizing the unfolding events in your mind, you hear your own inner voice articulating the written words, this phenomenon can be referred to as sub vocalization. Numerous researchers and experts in speed-reading contend that the act of sub vocalization impedes an individual's capacity to assimilate information at an accelerated pace. Their attention is excessively fixated on the singular word, thereby neglecting to fully comprehend the overarching concept that the words aim to articulate. It would be akin to endeavoring to vocalize each individual letter contained in this paragraph as opposed to comprehending the words collectively. The process of reciting each individual letter would consume considerably more time compared to reading each individual word.

Consequently, this decrease in sub vocalization accelerates their inherent reading pace. The pen, pencil, or stylus, when utilized, serves the purpose of directing attention to a particular section, thereby diverting focus away from the intellect and redirecting it onto the surface of the page. When individuals engage in the act of reading, they absorb the content and strive to grasp its meaning by constructing their own mental imagery. Recall the process we previously discussed in which children attempt to mentally reconstruct a story visually, thereby retaining the content within their memory? This principle is similarly utilized in adulthood, and it is this very principle that impedes the progress of numerous individuals in their acquisition of speed reading skills. Employing a pacer, such as a digit or a palm, can redirect one's attention towards the text, allowing the reader to enhance their cognitive capacity in assimilating ideas more expediently.

The singular detriment of this speed-reading technique lies in the fact that it prompts the eye to merely skim through the textual content, thereby markedly diminishing one's capacity for comprehension and retention of information. Consequently, this may result in overlooking significant and germane details contained within the text at hand. Therefore there\'s still an emphasis on viewing each and every word, even though it happens briefly. The process unfolds as follows: one must position their finger at the uppermost section of the page and progressively glide it downwards, endeavoring to maintain its course. One must assimilate all available information and subsequently revisit the starting point to visually trace either an "S" or a "Z." These motion patterns facilitate lateral eye movements across the entire page, helping to identify any individual words that may have been overlooked during the initial reading process.

An alternative approach in the realm of rapid reading is referred to as "skimming." This method entails quickly scanning the sentences on a page of written material with one's eyes, aiming to identify key indicators or insights that convey the intended message. For certain individuals, this ability is instinctive, whereas for most, it is typically gained through diligent practice. For instance, if one were to peruse the contents of a randomly selected college course textbook, it would become apparent that certain words within the text are emphasized by means of bold typography. This represents the fundamental concept of skimming. The mind assimilates these words, inherently comprehends their meaning through previously acquired knowledge, and can synthesize their general definitions to infer the content of the page.

Therefore, in the event that one were to unfold the pages of a textbook and encounter the terms "forensic," "medicine," "crime scene," and "gunshot," it can be reasonably inferred that said page pertains to the discourse of forensic techniques employed during investigations at crime scenes involving firearms and victims.

Furthermore, there exists an alternative technique in the evaluation of speed, known as "scanning." Some individuals employ this method by actively generating a mind-map to comprehend the information presented on the page. This mind-map facilitates the visualization of a hierarchical structure that organizes the scanned information in such a way as to establish relationships between the fundamental ideas presented in the text. Moreover, it illuminates the inherent interconnections between the various pieces of information, thereby effectively bolstering the ability to recall it at a later time. This represents the amalgamation of rapid information consumption, efficient organization, and robust retention within one's memory, thereby exemplifying the aptitude for speed reading.

As a case in point, suppose you have identified the aforementioned forensic countermeasure terms in the preceding illustration. In such a scenario, your next step would involve extracting each principal idea from the sentences containing those terms and establishing an interconnected correlation. The statement containing the term "forensic" possibly referred to the forensic safeguards employed by the suspect to mask their identity, whereas the sentence containing the word "gunshot" might allude to the underlying factor leading to the individual's demise. Consequently, it is possible to visualize both scenarios by acknowledging the following correlation between the sentences: despite the doctor's successful determination of the cause of death, the suspect's implementation of forensic measures prevented the doctor from obtaining any clues that could assist the detectives.

This illustrates the practice of not only comprehensively analyzing the sentences for their overarching significance but also establishing connections between the two elements, which ultimately improves the ability to retain and recall information at a later point in the case.

The SQ3R method is another technique employed to enhance retention and comprehension in speed reading. This acronym represents the methodology known as SQRRR, which comprises the sequential steps of surveying, questioning, reading, reciting, and reviewing. Authored by Francis Pleasant Robinson in 1946, the book Effective Study elucidated the methodology behind this approach by dissecting the precise manner in which the five steps are to be employed when applying diverse speed reading techniques.

The initial stage of the process involves conducting a survey, which entails briefly examining the text. It advises individuals to exercise restraint in reading an entire book, but rather suggests perusing the initial chapter or section and attentively documenting headings, subheadings, prominent words in bold, and any other noteworthy textual elements. It is estimated that you will require approximately 3 to 4 minutes for this task, which provides a preliminary overview of the content that can be anticipated from the current text. This is an opportune moment to mentally formulate any specific inquiries that the headings, subheadings, and notable characteristics may instigate within you.

Next, we proceed to interrogate. The inquiries that you are commencing to formulate serve as the foundation for this particular stage. The queries you construct ought to be grounded in the headings or subheadings observed, as these are the inquiries that will assist in staying focused while discerning the principal motifs within the text being perused. Inquiries such as, "What is the central theme of this chapter?", and "In what way does this information contribute to my understanding?" will also serve to facilitate your progress through the text; thus, do not hesitate to pose such questions and earnestly seek responses.

Once more, it is imperative that this step is executed within a timeframe of no more than 3 or 4 minutes before proceeding to the subsequent stage of this reading comprehension phase.

At present, it is opportune to engage in reading. Drawing upon the preliminary groundwork that has already been undertaken, engage in a passive examination of the material before you. Examine the material visually while reducing any internal speech and simply perform the actions without immediate cognitive processing. Initially, it may prove challenging, but it remains true that your eyes convey information to your brains, regardless of whether you consciously strive to create visual representations.

Next, we proceed to the "recitation" phase. In this context, the reader is expected to engage in a cognitive exercise, wherein they draw upon their memory to recollect and assimilate the acquired knowledge, as though they were endeavoring to impart it to another individual. It is imperative to comprehend, at this juncture, that proficiency in the retention and processing of this kind of information is acquired through consistent practice. Initially, your recollection may be limited, but there is no cause for concern. However, it is imperative to express the information that you can recollect using your own language. Your primary objective should be to concentrate on the key elements, while your ultimate objective is to achieve an encompassing overview of the entire text. The choice of conveying your thoughts through verbal means or documenting them in written form is at your own discretion; however, it is essential to note that opting for written documentation will significantly lengthen the duration of this particular phase of the procedure.

The final phase of this process entails conducting a review. In order to comprehend the information presented, it is advisable to revisit the content by engaging in a process of reading the chapter once more, in a reflective manner, with the intention of thoroughly reviewing the material before reaching its conclusion. Subsequently, endeavor to articulate the principal ideas to oneself once again, carefully synthesizing and restating in one's own language the information that has been recollected and retained from this specific chapter or section of the text. Please bear in mind that, at the initiation of this process, only discrete portions of chapters and texts will be effective. Nevertheless, as you persist in employing the approach, you will ascend in terms of information assimilation and gain the ability to implement the identical procedure with substantial segments of content encompassing numerous pages.

This is where the aspect of speed reading becomes relevant, however, it necessitates the systematic development of this technique from its fundamentals in order to achieve proficiency in it.

This approach is highly effective and yields remarkable results, leading numerous educational systems to adopt this strategy of information processing within their classrooms. The purpose behind this adoption is to facilitate students' comprehension and retention of the presented material. Although originally designed for higher education students, it is currently being utilized with a target age group as young as eight.

A variety of alternative techniques have been devised based on this fundamental approach, including the KWL table and the PQRST method. However, it is worth noting that neither of these approaches can match the efficacy of the aforementioned SQ3R method.

Nevertheless, it should not be assumed that the ability to read quickly equates to a comprehensive understanding of the advantageous applications and the overarching advantageous impact that speed reading can have on one's life. Fortunately, we are here to provide you with precise guidance on how the skill of speed reading can be beneficial not only to you, but also to any professional trajectory you may pursue in your life.

www.ingramcontent.com/pod-product-compliance
Lightning Source LLC
Chambersburg PA
CBHW050241120526
44590CB00016B/2179